There are many responsibilities and challenges that come when taking care of a duck in the city. Many funny and serious situations present themselves providing opportunities to learn how to overcome the obstacles in life.

Set in a new community in a large city, this story uses humor and adventure to teach the reader that hard work and determination pay off and that a duck can be a boy's best friend.

## A Note from the Author

In March 2020, my good friend, Jennifer Young and I, found ourselves in lock down due to the COVID -19 Pandemic. Jennifer told me that during her time in lock down, she was going to finish illustrating my book. Following her example, I dusted off the manuscript that had sat untouched for fifteen years! With 'fresh eyes' and all the time I needed; I was able to smooth out the rough edges to produce the final draft. Just before we were both called back to work, Jennifer and I met to insert her amazing artwork in between the pages of the manuscript!

# Acknowledgements

   Special thanks first and foremost goes to my friends/co-workers who encouraged me to write down all the tales I shared with them about raising a duckling.  Their enthusiasm gave me the courage and confidence to begin to write.  When I knew I was in over my head, another friend told me about the Institute of Children's Literature.  Over the course of a year, my final project, "A Web-Footed Friend," was down on paper.  Thanks again to these same friends who endured reading and re-reading all the many drafts.  As a tribute to you, I have used many of your names for the characters in the book.

   My special thanks to Jennifer Young.  Her talented illustrations really brought the book to life. Without her motivation, this book would still be a manuscript gathering dust.

   Last, but not least, my gratitude goes to my son Jacob.  Using all his computer skills, he has refined our work and has spent countless hours to upload the book onto the self-publishing site at Amazon.com.

## Chapter

1. Last Chance
2. Home at Last
3. The Final Verdict
4. The Clumsy Duckling
5. Bad Hair Day
6. Birthday Surprise
7. Knock. Knock. Who's There?
8. Backyard Buddies
9. Last One In!
10. A Web-Footed Friend
11. The Lazy Days of Summer
12. Back to School
13. A Trip to the Farm
14. Winter Quarters
15. Home Sweet Home
16. The Christmas Duck

# A Web-Footed Friend

Written by Marilyn Sabey
Illustrated by Jennifer Young

## Chapter One
**Last Chance**

    The scent of new leaves drifted in the air. Andy Johnson ran down the steep dirt path through the ravine behind his house on his way to Highwood Elementary School. He climbed up the other side of the ravine and stopped at the top to catch his breath. Looking back,

Andy noticed the trees had come alive in several brilliant shades of green.

"At least today is Friday," he thought and smiled. "Summer holidays will be here soon, and I will be playing outside instead of sitting in a classroom!"

Instantly his smile faded. His brows slanted, creasing his forehead into a familiar pattern of worry lines.

"Time is running out," he thought. "Somehow I have to convince Mom."

In the distance, several friends called to him from the school playground, but he did not feel like playing.

The bell rang and Andy hurried down the bustling halls to his fifth-grade classroom. As he entered the room, he heard the familiar cheeping coming from the large box at the back.

"Good morning, Duckworth," Andy said as he scooped up the tiny yellow duckling. All his worries melted away as he stroked the noisy ball of the fluff. "I'm happy to see you too."

Andy's smile broadened as Duckworth cheeped louder.

"Class let's get started," Miss Reed called out.

Andy quickly returned Duckworth to his box and took his seat. He thought Miss Reed was the coolest teacher in the school. Maybe it was because she was the youngest and the prettiest. She had a way of making everything fun and exciting.

"As you know class, our science project is now complete," she explained while sitting on the edge of her desk. "Hatching and caring for our duckling has been a wonderful learning experience for all of us. We had a lot of fun too. We will miss our little duckling."

Andy's heart sank. He knew what Miss Reed was going to say next.

"Mr. Sanders just told me this morning that Duckworth can go to live on his cousin's farm."

"Not Mr. Sanders," Andy thought. "I'm the only one who knows his plan. This is my last chance to save Duckworth!"

Andy shot his hand up into the air.

"Yes, Andy?" Miss Reed asked.

"Can I take Duckworth home instead?" Andy blurted out. His heart beat so fast that it was hard for him to speak. "Yeah, uh, Mom finally said I could keep him. She wrote you a note, but I forgot it at home. I'll bring it on Monday."

"That's great Andy!" Miss Reed replied with a huge smile. "I was hoping one of you would be able to take Duckworth home so that we can keep track of how he is doing."

"Can Andy bring him back for a visit?" asked another student.

I'm sure that could be arranged." Miss Reed replied. "Andy, I will give your Mom a quick call after school just to make sure she hasn't changed her mind. Now we better get to work. Get out your Math books and turn to page 98."

Andy finally took a breath. He couldn't believe it. Duckworth was coming home with him today! But what was even harder to believe, was that he had just lied to his favorite teacher. Instantly, he felt sick.

Chapter Two
**Home at Last**

"When did your Mom decide that you could keep Duckworth?" Matt asked as he and Andy struggled to get the awkward cardboard box through the front doors of the school. Matt Walker was Andy's best friend. He knew he could trust him with anything.

"She hasn't yet," Andy said quietly.

"But you told Miss Reed…"

"I had to," Andy snapped. "Just help me get Duckworth out of here. I'll explain everything on the way home."

"Well, I hope this explains why you've been acting so weird lately," Matt said.

Persistent protests could be heard from inside the box. Duckworth was obviously upset with the rough ride he was getting.

"Hold on, little guy," Andy answered. "We'll be home in no time."

They carried the box at an odd angle as they made their way down the steep path into the ravine. Finally, they reached the bottom.

"After school last week, I overheard Miss Reed talking to Mr. Sanders," Andy said. "They didn't know I was still in the hall. Miss Reed was telling him we were having trouble finding a home for Duckworth. Mr. Sanders said he would ask his cousin if he would be interested. His cousin lives on a farm."

"So, what's wrong with that?" Matt asked.

"When Mr. Sanders left the room, I hid behind the door." Andy explained. "As he walked down the hall, I heard him laugh and say to himself that he would have just enough time to fatten up that duck up for Christmas dinner!"

"That stinks!" Matt said. "Why didn't you tell Miss Reed?"

"I thought I would get into trouble." Andy said.

"You're going to be in real trouble when Miss Reed calls your Mom. What if she's talking to her right now?"

"She can't be. Mom isn't home."

"Didn't you tell Miss Reed...?" Matt started to say.

Andy interrupted. "It will be fine. I'll bring her a note on Monday."

"I can't believe you!" Matt said shaking his head. They started slowly climbing up the other side of the ravine. When they reached the top, they stood for a moment to shift the box and then they went through the back gate of the Johnson's backyard.

"What now?" Matt asked.

"Let's put him in the garden shed." Andy opened the old wooden door and the boys pushed the box inside.

"There you go, Duckworth," Andy said peeking inside the lid of the box. "We are home at last."

Duckworth looked a little ruffled from the trip home; his soft yellow down wet and matted with food pellets. His bill was open slightly as if he were out of breath.

Andy closed the shed door. "You'll be safe here."

"I've got to go," Matt said as they walked around the side of the house. "Good luck, Andy."

"Thanks, Matt! I'll call you later."

Andy unlocked the front door. He had made it. The phone rang. "It was probably Miss Reed," he thought. Andy removed his shoes and backpack, threw his coat over the bannister and ran down the hall into the family room. He did a flying leap onto the couch then turned on the T.V. Thankfully the phone stopped ringing just as he heard his mom come in the front door and walk down the hall.

"Hi, Andy," Helen Johnson said. "How was your day?" she asked and sat down motioning Andy to join her.

"I scored three goals playing soccer at recess," Andy told his Mom. "At lunch, Ben Wood launched his chocolate pudding across the room."

"I hope you don't do anything like that," Helen said.

"Don't worry, Mom. I'm not that stupid. Ben got into so much trouble."

Then Andy remembered the lies he had told and felt ashamed.

Ryan, Andy's 17-year-old brother, bolted into the kitchen. "Hey, when is supper?" Ryan constantly thought about food.

"Dad will be home in an hour," Mom said checking something in the oven. "Do either of you have homework?" Ryan shook his head.

"I have just a few math questions," Andy said, "but they won't take me long." He got his backpack and ran up the stairs to his room.

Math was the last thing on Andy's mind. "I have to get Duckworth out of the shed," he thought. "It's cold and dark in there. Mom and Dad just have to let me keep him." Suddenly a look of horror crossed Andy's face. "What if Miss Reed finds out that I lied?

## Chapter Three
## The Final Verdict

    Andy was so distracted he soon gave up on his homework. He grabbed the bag of duck food and water bottle out of his backpack and quietly crept down the stairs. In his hurry to get out the front door, he ran right into Sara, his 14-year-old sister.
    "Where are you going?" she asked while flipping her long hair over her shoulder.
    "Nowhere," Andy said hiding the food behind his back. Sara gave him a strange look and went into the house. Andy walked around to the shed. Duckworth was quiet until Andy opened the door. Then he cheeped desperately and tried to jump out of the box.

"You don't like it in here, do you?" Andy said softly while he stroked the little duck. "I see you cleaned yourself up. Here's some food and water."

"Come and eat," Andy's mother called through the small kitchen window.

"I'll be back later, Duckworth." Andy shut the shed door and ran into the house. He was the last one to get to the table. As usual, Ryan had already started eating.

"You're late, kid," he said with a mouth full of food.

"Hi, Andy," Carl Johnson said looking up over his glasses. "How was school?"

"Good, Dad."

"So, where did you go just before dinner?" Sara asked.

"Why do older sisters have to be so nosy?" Andy questioned.

"I just asked where you were," Sara said.

Andy quickly changed the subject.

"Mom I talked to Chris from down the street about getting a flyer route. His route is too big for one person and he said I can take over half of it. It will pay forty dollars a month. I can start Monday."

"That's great, Andy," Mom replied. "Ryan and Sara had a flyer route a few years ago. Remember?"

"It was pretty good money," Ryan said between bites, "until Sara got us fired."

"Well, it was cold outside, and I wanted to get home," Sara said defensively. "I didn't think anyone would notice the flyers I tossed over the fence into the ravine."

This was not the way Andy wanted the conversation to go, so he started again.

"Anyway, with the money, I could easily take care of Duckworth."

"Oh, here we go again." Ryan said reaching for another bun. "Mom, just let him have the duck."

"It's not that easy, Ryan. It's a big responsibility. What will you feed him?" Mom inquired.

"United Farmers Association sells duck pellets. Miss Reed said it only costs seven dollars for a fifty-pound bag," Andy said excitedly.

"Not bad," Dad commented.

This is going better, Andy thought to himself. "So, I can have the duck?" he asked holding his breath. All eyes were on Mom and Dad.

"Well," Dad hesitated, "where will he live?"

"He can live on the deck...until he gets bigger, then in the backyard."

"What about Pugsley?" Sara asked. Pugsley was Sara's rabbit.

"I'm sure a duck and a rabbit can share our big back yard," Andy said calmly.

"Just for the record, I am not cleaning up after any duck," Ryan said.

"Me either," Sara added.

"I'll do all the work," Andy said. "Come on Mom. Dad. Remember the stories you told us about the baby animals that you brought home and raised. I can do it too."

"Let him have the duck so we don't have to listen to him anymore," Sara pleaded.

"You're not about to give up on this one, are you?" Dad asked.

"No." Andy shook his head. "Please?"

"What do you think, Carl?" Mom looked across the table at Dad. Andy took in a deep breath. This would be the final verdict!

"I'd say the boy has done his homework," Dad said. "I admire a person who works through a problem logically to find the solution."

"Well, Mom?" Andy asked trying to control his excitement.

"Okay. Okay," she laughed.

"Thank you, thank you! I promise I won't disappoint you." Andy jumped up from his chair to give his parents a hug. "I'll go get Duckworth right now." He ran to the back door. Everyone at the table looked confused.

"The school is closed now," Mom called after him.

"I'll bet the duck is already here," Sara sneered.

## Chapter Four
## **The Clumsy Duckling**

Andy opened the shed and reached inside the box.  Duckworth cheeped with delight.

"Here we go buddy," Andy said picking him up.  The duckling felt warm and soft.  "Be on your best behavior.  Try not to make a mess, or, at least, not until they fall in love with you."

Andy carried Duckworth into the house.

"This is Duckworth," Andy said as he carefully lowered the little yellow ball of fluff onto the floor.

"He's so small," Mom said.  "He's only the size of a baseball."

"What kind of duck is he?" Dad asked.

"He is a Peking duck," Andy said. "They came from China. Our class studied about them. The first ones were brought to America by a ship that arrived at New York City in 1873."

"Look at his big webbed feet! They're light pink! So is his bill. Aren't they supposed to be orange?" Sara asked.

"Not until he gets older," Andy replied.

Duckworth took a few steps and tripped.

"His feet are too big for his body. He has to stand with one on top of the other one," Ryan said. "He looks like he might tip over from the weight of his huge bill!"

"You two make a good pair, Andy," Sara smiled. "You need to grow into a few things too. Like your ears."

Duckworth started cheeping. "It's okay." Andy stroked his back. The duckling instantly calmed down. "Feel how soft his down is."

"When will he get his feathers?" Mom asked raising her voice so she could be heard over the constant cheeping.

"He's three weeks old now, so he will probably have all his white feathers in another two months," Andy answered.

"I thought ducks were supposed to quack," Sara said.

"He will, when he is about four months old. Except, it won't really sound like the quack you normally think of. Those are the hens, or females. Duckworth is a drake, a male, so he'll make a long 'wongh' sound. We heard them in a movie. It's not as loud."

"I'm amazed at how much you know about ducks," Dad said. "I'm proud of you, son."

"Thanks, Dad. We did a lot of reading about them in class."

"Why does he keep cheeping?" Ryan asked.

"He's probably hungry." Andy walked down the hallway toward the kitchen. Duckworth quickly waddled behind him with his feet slapping loudly on the tiled floor.

Andy poured duck pellets onto a plate and water into a small bowl. As soon as Andy placed the food and water onto the kitchen floor, Duckworth dove in. He picked up the pellets in his bill so quickly that many of them sprinkled across the floor. Then he dipped his bill into the water and tipped his head back to swallow.

"The food has to be wet so he can swallow it," Andy said. "He is a messy eater."

"That's an understatement," exclaimed Mom. Duckworth continued to eat ravenously. "He looks like he hasn't eaten for a week."

Soon all the food was gone or at least off the plate. There was a lot in the bottom of the water dish and on the floor. Duckworth stepped back and stretched.

"Are those his wings?" Ryan pointed to the one-inch stubs that appeared from under the yellow down. Duckworth tried to flap his little wings which caused him to lose his balance. His oversized foot caught on the edge of the water bowl spilling out what was left. Then the clumsy little duckling wobbled around until he finally regained his balance. Everyone roared with laughter. He ran through the puddle of water, mixing the spilled food on the floor into a yucky mush. Andy reached for the nearest towel to clean up.

"Not with that!" Mom yelled at Andy. It was too late. He was already mopping up the mess with her fancy kitchen towel. Andy realized his mistake and quickly pulled the towel away, knocking Duckworth over onto his back. Both his feet were kicking and flicking the mush everywhere.

"Did any of those books tell you how messy ducks are?" Sara asked rolling her eyes.

## Chapter Five
## Bad Hair Day

Andy stood at the kitchen sink rinsing the rags he used to clean up the floor.

"When you are finished, make sure you clean out the sink."

"Sure, Mom," Andy answered. "Take a look at Duckworth." Tired out from the day's events, Duckworth was curled up and asleep on top of Andy's feet.

"He sure likes you," Mom said laughing. "Did you notice that the minute you were out of Duckworth's sight, he would start calling for you?"

"He thinks I'm his Mom," Andy stated proudly.

"Isn't that called imprinting?" Mom asked.

"Yes, we watched a movie at school about a wild duckling who was abandoned and imprinted on the lady that looked after him. Even after he was full grown, he would follow her everywhere. The duck would even fly beside her car when she was driving."

"Wow, that's really something," Mom exclaimed.

"Too bad Duckworth won't ever fly," Andy said sadly. "Domestic ducks can't fly because of the way they have been bred."

When Andy finished cleaning, he scooped up the warm ball of fluff and went into the family room. Duckworth sat in Andy's lap on an old towel. Andy told his parents about Mr. Sanders and the lie he told to Miss Reed. Mom said lying was never a good idea but given the same situation, she probably would have done the same thing. Dad agreed. Andy was relieved that they understood. He felt much better.

"That's one tired duck," Dad said reaching for the newspaper. "It's been a big day for both of you."

"Do you think I could bring his box into the kitchen for a few days until he gets used to things?" Andy asked.

"I guess so," Mom consented.

"But only for a couple of days," Dad added cautiously.

"Mom, do you want to hold him while I get it?" After all the stories she had told them about her pets, Andy knew she wouldn't be able to resist. He could hear her speaking softly to Duckworth as he left the house to get the box.

The weekend flew by. Soon Andy learned to play with Duckworth in the kitchen before he fed him, that way the duckling was less excited and there were fewer accidents. Cleaning up was easier.

Andy woke up early each morning so he could spend time with Duckworth before he went to school. Duckworth seemed happy to go back in his box and sleep while Andy was at school. Andy ran home most days for lunch and hurried home after school as well.

By the middle of the week, Andy moved Duckworth's box outside the kitchen door onto the deck. Even though Andy did all he could, the box was constantly a mess and had to be replaced with new ones.

After Andy's flyers were delivered, he and Duckworth would hang out in the kitchen for the evening. Duckworth would spend hours pulling and cleaning the tiny white feathers that were coming in on his breast and tail. Every night he would fall asleep on Andy's feet while Andy did his homework or watched T.V.

At bedtime, Andy put Duckworth in his box with a big bowl of food and every morning it was gone. At this rate, Andy would need more food by the weekend. Duckworth was getting bigger each day.

When school ended on Friday, Andy was exhausted. He trudged slowly up the hill and into his backyard. As usual, he went straight to Duckworth's box on the deck. Duckworth cheeped with excitement as Andy picked him up.

"Hi, little guy," Andy said. "Pretty soon I won't be able to call you that. You're getting so big."

Sara came out onto the deck. "Hey, do you want to introduce Duckworth to Pugsley?" she asked.

Andy hesitated. "I guess so."

"Here, Pugsley. Here, bunny!" Sara called in a silly high-pitched voice. Pugsley was the only rabbit Andy knew that would come when called.

Within seconds, the white and gray Miniature Holland Lop hopped out from under the deck. She was half the size of a regular rabbit. She had big floppy ears that drooped down almost to her feet and a tiny pink nose that was constantly twitching.

"Pugsley, this is Duckworth," Sara said. Andy carried the little duck into the yard and carefully placed him on the grass.

"He's still smaller than Pugsley," Andy said anxiously.

Pugsley hopped over to see the newcomer. Duckworth backed up then ran in between Andy's legs.

"He's scared," Andy said scooping up the duck. Pugsley started to run in circles around Andy and Duckworth.

"She just wants to play," Sara said disappointed.

"Maybe once he is older, we can try again," Andy said.

Andy put Duckworth on the trampoline and climbed on to lay down. Pugsley ran back under the deck and Sara went into the house.

Duckworth snuggled right beside Andy's head. "Doesn't the warm sun feel good?"

Duckworth was already busy cleaning his feathers. The soft down felt good brushing against Andy's cheek as Duckworth pulled his feathers through his bill. The gentle repetitive motion soon put Andy to sleep.

Once Duckworth finished with his feathers, he started on Andy's hair. Taking a small clump of hair at the roots, Duckworth pulled the strands through his bill. He continued working up the side of Andy's head. The saliva from the duck's mouth made Andy's hair stand on end.

"Andy! It's supper time," Mom called from the back door.

Andy woke up, startled. He didn't realize he had slept so long. Luckily Duckworth was still beside him.

"You were a good boy while I was sleeping," Andy said as he carried him up to the deck.

The family was already seated at the table. As soon as Andy entered the kitchen everyone roared with laughter.

"What happened to your hair?" Sara gasped.

"What do you mean?" Andy's confused look turned to surprise as he touched his hair. It was hard and standing up!

"Your hair looks like the pins in a pin cushion," Mom commented.

"Duckworth must have done your hair while you were sleeping!" Sara cried.

"You're having a really bad hair day," Ryan teased.

## Chapter Six
### The Birthday Surprise

    Saturday morning Matt came over to see Andy.

    "Wow, I think Duckworth has grown since I saw him two days ago!" exclaimed Matt.

    "I know. It's like he grows overnight. See his new feathers," Andy boasted.

    "I think he is louder too," Matt yelled above the constant cheeping.

    "He settles down once he's out for a while, but he never lets me out of his sight. He hates to be left alone unless he's in his box." Andy opened the kitchen door and Duckworth waddled into the kitchen right behind him. "He'll follow me anywhere." Andy ran down the hall and back with Duckworth cheeping at his heels.

"Watch this!" Andy hid in the pantry. Duckworth looked around for Andy but could not see him so immediately he called out in a panic. Andy slowly poked his head out. Duckworth spotted Andy and ran to him cheeping non-stop.

"That's so cool," Matt said amazed. "Well, I better go. I wish I could stay longer, but I have to help out at my sister's birthday party. Hey, why don't you surprise Becky and bring Duckworth to her party?"

"I don't know…" Andy started to reply.

"Come on, it will be fun," Matt coaxed. "Come around noon."

In the meantime, Ryan drove Andy to the United Farmers Association to get more food for Duckworth. Ryan passed his driver's test recently and was happy to drive anyone just about anywhere.

"It's a good thing his food is cheap," Andy commented. "He eats so much."

"Why don't you by two bags so you don't have to come back as often?" Ryan suggested.

"Good idea," Andy said as they pulled into the store's parking lot.

"This is sure different from any store I've been to," Ryan commented as they walked in.

There were bridles, harnesses and reins for horses, feeding troughs, salt licks, cattle prods, all kinds of gardening equipment and even huge lawn mowers that looked like small tractors. Covering one entire wall was a large board listing all the different kinds of feed.

"Can I help you?" asked the clerk.

"Yes, please. I need some duckling food."

"How many ducks do you have and how old are they?" the clerk inquired.

"Oh, just one duck and he's a month and a half old," Andy answered feeling kind of silly.

"Okay, you'll need one bag of duckling mix. Feed it to him until it's gone," the clerk smiled. "You can give him poultry mix after that."

Andy paid for a bag of each mix.

"Take this receipt and drive around to the big storage building at the back to pick it up," the clerk instructed.

"I guess this must be a pretty small order compared to what most farmers buy," Ryan said. "Come on, Farmer Andy. Let's go pick it up."

As they left the store, Ryan started singing, "And on his farm he had a duck, eee-yi-eee-yi-oh."

Just before noon, Andy arrived at Matt's house with Duckworth tucked inside a sports bag slung over his shoulder. By the sound of it, the house was filled with giggling seven-year-old girls.

"You wait here in the laundry room until everyone gathers in the kitchen to sing Happy Birthday," Matt whispered. "I'll come get you when it is time."

Andy unzipped the bag just enough to let Duckworth poke his head out. Duckworth was panting through his slightly opened bill.

"I'm sorry that you're upset," Andy spoke softly. "We'll say happy birthday and then go home, I promise."

Almost immediately Matt came back. "Come on, let's go."

Andy followed Matt into the kitchen. The girls were all seated at the table waiting to cut the cake.

"Hi, Andy," Mrs. Walker said. "Girls, I can't find the candles. I'll be right back."

"Hey, Andy, aren't you going to wish me a happy birthday?" Becky screeched with excitement. Her friends giggled for no reason.

"Andy has a surprise for your birthday," Matt raised his voice to get everyone's attention.

"What is it? What is it?" Becky begged.

Andy walked slowly to the table as the girls watched with quiet anticipation. Andy reached into his bag and pulled out Duckworth.

"He's so cute!" they cried all together.

"Look at his feet."

"He looks so soft."

"Can we hold him?"

All this attention scared Duckworth to death. Andy lost his hold and the duck plunged feet first into the birthday cake! Duckworth flapped his tiny wings and tried to move. The harder he tried the deeper he sank into the cake until he fell over on top of it.

Everyone, except Becky, laughed as Duckworth lifted his bill out of the icing.

"My cake!" Becky screamed.

Andy pulled Duckworth off the cake and wrestled the sticky duck back into the bag. Duckworth flicked the icing off his bill and onto the girls. They screamed and laughed even harder.

"You're scaring the duck!" Andy cried but no one could hear him. Andy put the bag down on the floor to zip it up. Duckworth jumped out and ran as fast as a duck with sticky feet can go, leaving a trail of icing across the kitchen floor.

"I found the candles," Mrs. Walker said as she walked back into the kitchen. She looked up and gasped. "What happened to the cake?"

Suddenly everyone was silent. Matt looked up sheepishly at his Mom, "Surprise!?"

## Chapter Seven
### Knock. Knock. Who's There?

"Sorry I can't stay, Matt," Andy said. "I need to get home and clean Duckworth before the icing dries."

"That's okay," Matt replied. "This whole thing was a bad idea."

"Well, at least you didn't get in too much trouble."

"Yeah, after Mom said she was leaving to buy another cake, Becky said it was the best birthday surprise she's ever had," Matt commented.

"It's one she'll never forget," Andy said. "None of us will, especially your Mom."

As soon as Andy got home, he put Duckworth into the bathroom sink. Immediately Duckworth started to play in the water.

"You don't mind this at all, do you?" Andy asked as he washed the icing off Duckworth's bill. "When you get a little bigger, I'll buy you a swimming pool."

Once Duckworth was cleaned up, Andy took him out on the deck. The duck protested when Andy tried to put him in the box.

"I guess you are getting too big to stay in there. Maybe it's time for you to hang out on the deck during the day. At night I'll put you in your box to sleep."

Andy tipped the box on its side, so Duckworth could go in and out as he pleased. He shut the gate on the deck, so Duckworth was safely enclosed inside.

"Here's your food and water," Andy said. "I'm going inside now to do my homework."

When Andy opened the door, Duckworth rushed in after him.

"You stay out here," Andy said. "I'm tired of cleaning up after you."

Andy felt terrible shutting him out on the deck. Duckworth called and called as he walked back and forth in front of the French doors. When it was clear that he was not going to settle down, Andy went to the door and tapped the glass.

"I'm right here Duckworth," Andy said sadly. "You're just too big to stay in the house. It's too hard to clean up after you."

When Duckworth saw Andy through the glass door, he nodded his head and cheeped in relief. Andy sat in the kitchen chair closest to the door to do his homework so Duckworth could see him. The duck eventually settled down and went to sleep.

When Duckworth woke up and noticed Andy was gone, he panicked and started to call. Andy heard him calling from his bedroom which overlooked the deck. He ran down the stairs and rushed out to see him.

"I'm here, ducky," Andy said.

Duckworth cheeped with delight. Andy stayed and played with him until it was time for supper. Then he shut him out on the deck again. Just like before, Duckworth called and called. Andy was so tired and frustrated he wanted to cry.

"What's wrong, son?" Dad asked.

"I've decided it's time to leave Duckworth out on the deck," Andy sobbed. "But he's scared to be out there by himself and he keeps calling for me. I can't stand to see him so upset. I don't want him to think that I'm abandoning him."

"Well, I think you've made the right decision," Dad said. "Duckworth will adjust. Just give him some time. The next few weeks will probably be harder for you than it will be for the duck.

Andy's Dad was right. At the end of the second week, Duckworth stopped calling when he was left alone.

"Duckworth seems much happier now," Andy said at supper. "Most of the time he is content just looking through the door at us. Whenever he sees us, he nods his head like he's greeting us."

"Well, I'm glad to see that you are much happier," Mom said.

"So am I," Ryan added. "You did a lot of sniveling in the last two weeks."

"I think we've got Duckworth trained," Andy sighed with relief.

"But if he can't see anyone," Mom said, "he still taps on the glass with his bill."

"It's like he is playing, Knock. Knock. Who's there?" Andy added. "When I hear him do that, I go to the door to see him."

"I do too," said Mom.

"I think we all do," Dad said.

"Well, do you know what I think?" Sara enquired. "I think that the duck has got you all trained!"

## Chapter Eight
## Backyard Buddies

Andy was happy to have Duckworth living on the deck, but he wasn't sure his family was.

"Annndyyyyy!" his dad roared.

"I'm coming!" Andy came running down the stairs. He knew what that tone of voice meant. When he got to the kitchen door, he found his father sprawled on the floor of the deck. Raw hamburger patties were scattered everywhere. Duckworth stood by his side, innocently eating one of the patties.

"I nearly broke my neck, all because of that duck!" Dad snapped. "Why does this duck have to be so messy?"

"I've been asking myself that same question, Dad," Andy replied. He didn't dare tell him that he had cleaned the deck twice already.

"So, what answer have you come up with?" Dad demanded as he got up slowly, trying to salvage the patties that were still on the plate.

"Well, it's because he eats so much," Andy stated, hoping this approach would work. "Did you know that the Peking duck is the fastest growing breed of all ducks, and the fastest breed to mature, in only six months?"

"That's all very interesting son, but it's not working. I'm going to have a shower and when I get back, this mess better be cleaned up!"

Andy put on rubber boots, opened the gate on the deck, and walked down the stairs into the backyard. He threw the hose onto the deck and turned it on.

"This is the third time today I've had to clean the deck," he complained as he stomped back up the stairs. Duckworth waddled through the water and picked up the hose with his bill. Andy got the rubber broom and pushed the water off the deck. Duckworth thought it was a game and chased after the broom. He slipped and fell onto his side with his feet kicking in the air. Clumsily, he got back on to his feet and flipped the hose with his bill, spraying water on Andy.

"It's a good thing that you're so cute," Andy said.

When he finished, he put the hose away and sat on the step. It was still wet, but Andy was too tired to care. Duckworth came over and stood beside him.

"What am I going to do with you?" Andy asked impatiently. Duckworth only nodded his head. To add to Andy's bad mood, he remembered Miss Reed wanted him to write a few paragraphs telling how Duckworth was doing and then present it to the class before summer holidays. His mind drifted over all the things he might say. Then he got an idea. "I'll write one paragraph as though you are speaking," he explained to Duckworth. Andy sat back and imagined what Duckworth might say:

"I finally figured out that life on the deck is pretty good. I really don't know what took me so long to figure it out. There's nothing like sleeping in the warm sun or smelling the fresh air! I love to watch my family through the kitchen door. If I want to see one of them, all I have to do is tap on the glass with my bill, and they come running. When it rains, I have puddles to play in! I can watch the birds up in the sky and even chase away the magpies who try to steal my food. Yup, this is the life!"

Andy smiled at Duckworth. "I bet the class will be glad to hear that you're so happy here. Now I'll tell my side of the story." Andy imagined himself in front of the class. He cleared his throat and said out loud:

"Boy, taking care of a duck is way harder than I thought it would be. At least he's out on the deck now so cleaning up after him is easier. But why does he have to be so messy?" Maybe it's because he eats so much! I've definitely learned one thing: What goes in must come out! I don't know why my family is so hyper about a little duck mess on the deck. My sister insists that the deck is cleaned first thing in the morning so she can put her rabbit in the backyard for the day. Mom complains if the deck isn't clean when she goes to the garden. My brother yells at me after school to clean the deck when he wants to go jump on the trampoline and Dad grumbles if there is any mess on the deck when he wants to use the barbeque. They just don't get it. I am cleaning the deck. I clean it four or five times a day! Yup, this is the life...of a Zookeeper!"

"I like it!' Andy said to Duckworth. "I'm going inside to write it down before I forget."

After Andy finished writing, he decided that things had to change.

"Sara," he called. "Let's try getting Pugsley and Duckworth together again."

"Okay," she answered. "I'll be out in a minute."

Andy raced into the backyard past his Dad who was barbequing the remaining hamburgers.

"Here, Pugsley. Here bunny!" Andy yelled trying to sound as ridiculous as Sara did when she called.

It worked. The rabbit came hopping out from under the deck.

"Wait for me," Sara said walking onto the deck. "Look Duckworth is bigger than Pugsley now!"

"Wow! He grew a lot in a month," Andy exclaimed.

"What if they don't get along?" Sara asked nervously.

"Let's see," Andy said placing Duckworth down onto the grass. This time Duckworth seemed quite interested and waddled over to see the rabbit. He nodded and cheeped softly. Pugsley wiggled her pink nose, and then hopped in a circle around Duckworth.

"Hey, Dad, look," Andy yelled. "They like each other."

Dad glanced up from the barbeque and smiled. Pugsley ran to the back fence and Duckworth followed right behind her. Andy and Sara watched Duckworth follow Pugsley around the backyard. When Dad called them for supper, they left Duckworth in the yard with Pugsley.

"So, where's the duck?" Ryan asked as he stuffed a hamburger into his mouth.

"He's in the backyard with Pugsley," Sara proclaimed.

"Do they get along? Mom asked.

"Yeah," Andy said with a grin. "They really like each other."

"Hey, does this mean there won't be any more mess on the deck?" Ryan asked enthusiastically.

"If all goes well, I may have just cleaned the deck for the last time!"

"That is good news," Dad sighed.

"I don't know," Mom said. "Now we'll have a mess all over the backyard."

"I was thinking of fencing off the side of the yard between the houses. Duckworth could stay there and sleep in the old fort we built under the deck." Andy suggested.

"Pugsley goes in there all the time," Sara said. "I was going to start leaving her outside at night, now that it's warmer. If they continue to get along, they could sleep there together."

"That's great," Andy said. "They can be backyard buddies!"

## Chapter Nine
## Last One In!

    Summer was approaching quickly and the next few days flew by. Duckworth and Pugsley were always together. Andy couldn't have been happier.
    "Everyone liked hearing about Duckworth today." Matt said on their way home from school.
    "They couldn't believe how much he grew," Andy commented.
    Andy and Matt talked non-stop about all the things they could do during the summer.
    "We should finish the fort in the ravine," Andy suggested.

"Sure," Matt agreed. "We need a new bike trail through the trees to get there."

"It would be fun to take Duckworth to the pond," Andy said.

They stopped and yelled across the ravine, "School's out for summer!"

"Hey, Duckworth," Andy bellowed as he and Matt opened the backyard gate. Duckworth came running to meet them with Pugsley hopping along behind.

"The first thing I want to do this summer is buy Duckworth a swimming pool," Andy said. "Let's go find Ryan. Maybe we can talk him into driving us to the store."

Ryan was in such a good mood after writing his last grade twelve exam that it didn't take much to convince him to go. They piled into Ryan's car and left for the store. Soon they returned with a blue kiddy pool tied on top of the car.

"Hurry," Ryan said. "Let's get this off my car before someone I know sees me."

Matt and Ryan were on the ends of the pool and Andy was in the middle underneath, using his head to hold it up.

"Good thing you're so short," Ryan teased. The three boys carried the pool into the backyard.

"Where do you want this thing?" Ryan asked.

"Over there, just off the deck by the bushes," Andy nodded.

"There you go," Ryan said. "I'll see you guys later."

"Thanks," Andy called after him.

Duckworth came out from under the deck to investigate. He nodded his head and then tapped the pool with his bill.

"Are you sure he's going to like it?" Matt asked.

"Once he sees the water, he will." Andy put the hose in the pool and turned it on. Duckworth waddled over for a closer look. "This is your pool, Ducky," Andy said. "Matt, help me put this big rock beside it so he can get in."

Once the pool was full, Andy splashed his hand in the water trying to coax Duckworth to get in.

"Look at him," Andy said. "He wants to get in, but he is not sure how." Andy placed him on the rock. "Come on, Duckworth, you can do it!"

Duckworth couldn't resist any longer. He threw himself over the edge of the pool and glided to the other side. He floated peacefully on the water, dipping his bill in, and then tipped it back to swallow. Then suddenly

Duckworth dunked his entire head under water splashing it up onto his back. He spread his tail to catch the water dripping down. With his wings slightly opened in the water, Duckworth repeated the motions over and over.

"He loves it!" Matt exclaimed.
With the help of his wings, Duckworth lowered his breast deep into the water while he pulled his head back, close to his body. He did this a couple of times and then, without any warning, he beat one wing on top of the water, followed immediately by the other wing, splashing water everywhere. Before the boys could move away, they were soaked.

"There won't be any water left in the pool if he keeps this up," Andy shouted over the loud splashing.

Suddenly Duckworth made a wild dash across the pool and dove under the water to the other side. Wildly flapping his wings, he scooted across the water and dove back again. Duckworth carried on plunging back and forth in the water then finally he came back to a stop.

"Wow, that looked like fun," Matt said. Duckworth struggled at the side of the pool.

"I don't think he can get out," Andy said. "Help me get another rock to put inside the pool."

As soon as the boys lowered the rock into the pool, Duckworth used his bill to pull himself on top of it.

"Yes!" Andy cheered.

Duckworth stayed on the rock and flapped the water off his wings and then shook his tail.

"Look, he's cleaning his feathers. Why does he need to do that if he just had a bath?" Matt asked.

"It's called 'preening'," Andy explained. "After a bath, a duck needs to get dry. That's why he did all that flapping and shaking. Now he pulls his feathers through his bill, collecting any water that might be left. Then he shakes his bill to get rid of the water."

"How do you know all this stuff?" Matt asked.

"I read about it," Andy replied. "Look how he's reaching his head back to his tail. There is an oil gland there." Duckworth gracefully rolled his head back and forth over the base of his tail. "Now he is arranging and oiling his feathers. The oil will make him waterproof and if the feathers lay properly, air will be trapped in the layers to keep him warm."

Duckworth reached back with his bill to pick up some oil, and then quickly pulled his feathers through his bill.

Andy and Matt watched Duckworth continue to preen for a long time.

"He sure likes his pool," Andy said. "I wonder if he will ever get out."

"Well you know the old saying," Matt said. "Like a duck to water!"

The first week of the summer holiday was disappointing. "When is it going to stop raining?" Andy grumbled as he looked out his bedroom window. "Duckworth is back in his pool again," he said to Matt. "He likes the rain."

"Well, at least somebody does," Matt moaned.

The boys watched Duckworth pull the overhanging leaves into the pool, then play with them in the water.

"Hey, we should go outside and look for worms," Andy suggested. "We can feed them to Duckworth."

"That sounds better that sitting here," Matt replied. "Let's go."

By the time the boys put on their jackets and got outside, Duckworth was out of the pool and waddling back and forth in a big puddle underneath the trampoline.

"He's looking for worms," Andy said. "He found one," Andy called out to Matt. "Did you see him eat it?"

"Yeah, he's really fast," Matt replied. "Look, he's pulling another one out of the ground! How can he hang on to something so slippery?"

"There's a small nail on the end of his bill that he uses to dig or grab things with," Andy explained. "He can really pinch with it. He's bruised me several times."

"He's got another worm," Matt said. Duckworth swallowed the worm in a flash, and then started looking for more. Matt and Andy searched the yard too. Soon they both had a handful of worms. They fed them to Duckworth who gobbled them down.

'It looks like he is eating spaghetti," Andy said. "Let's find some more."

When they came back to feed more worms to Duckworth, they found him playing in the mud.

"He's putting his whole head into the mud puddle," Andy said.

Duckworth stood up. Mud dripped off his face and bill, then onto his neck, down his breast and between his feet.

"What a dirty duck," Matt said. "Look, he's doing it again."

Duckworth repeated his comical routine over and over until he had a thick black line of mud running down the front of his body from head to toe.

"He looks like a skunk except backwards!" Andy said. He laughed so hard he slipped into the mud puddle. He rolled over and knocked Matt off his feet and into the mud. Duckworth thought it was a game and joined in the fun. Soon the three of them were covered in mud.

"Man, we better get cleaned up before Mom sees us," Andy remarked.

"Quick!' Matt yelled and pointed to the pool. "Last one in...is a dirty duck!"

## Chapter Ten
## A Web-Footed Friend

The weather finally cleared up. Andy and Matt spent their days outside with Duckworth or exploring the ravine.

One particularly hot day Mom asked Andy to put the sprinkler on the backyard. "It's been so hot, the grass is dying," she said.

"Sure, Mom," Andy answered. "As he walked into the backyard, Duckworth and Pugsley ran out from under the deck to greet him.

"Hi, you guys. Are you keeping cool under there?"

Duckworth made his usual nodding motion. He was almost full grown and far bigger than Pugsley now. He had become a beautiful white duck weighing about fifteen pounds. His bill and feet had turned bright orange and his tiny wings were now at least a meter across. He followed Andy to the side of the house and watched him twist the sprinkler onto the hose. Pugsley hopped over to see what was so interesting. Andy pulled the hose to the middle of the yard and set the sprinkler down. The animals following along behind him. He ran back to turn on the water. When the water sprayed out, Duckworth flapped his wings with excitement while Pugsley scurried under the deck for shelter. Duckworth waddled closer and closer to the sprinkler until the water hit his breast.

"Do you want to run through the sprinkler?" Andy asked, taking his shirt off. He ran past Duckworth, through the sprinkler, to the other side of the yard. Duckworth waddled after him, flapping his wings and cheeping loudly.

"I can't believe it, Mom! Sara!" Andy screamed with amazement. "Duckworth is running through the sprinkler with me."

This soon became one of their favorite pastimes on hot summer days. Andy and Duckworth also spent many days exploring the thick wooded area in the ravine. There were always good bugs there for Duckworth to eat. Once he even caught a mouse and ate it. Andy didn't tell anyone though. It was too gross.

One day, Andy wanted to take Pugsley along on their adventure.

"You're not taking Pugsley anywhere without me," Sara said as she put Pugsley's harness on and attached it to a leash.

Duckworth followed Andy, Pugsley hopped behind the duck, and Sara followed Pugsley.

"I bet we are quite a sight to see," Sara said.

"We won't go very far," Andy said. "Once we get to the first clump of trees, we'll stop. There's a neat log I want to take to the fort."

When they got there, Sara tied Pugsley's leash to a bush. Duckworth stayed close to the rabbit, poking his bill through the grass, trying to find bugs.  Pugsley enjoyed eating the leaves off a nearby bush.

"Can you come with me to get the log?" Andy asked.

Sara hesitated.  "And leave the animals alone?"

"It won't take long," Andy replied.  "They will be happy here for a while."

Andy had trouble finding the old log and they were about to give up, when they heard a dog barking.

"Duckworth!  Pugsley!" they called as they ran back.  Through the last few trees, they could see a dog trying to get near Pugsley.  Duckworth was between Pugsley and the dog.  His head was down near the ground.  The feathers on his back were puffed up and his wings were slightly spread.  He moved slowly toward the dog making a hissing sound.  The dog jumped forward.  Duckworth quickly raised his head striking the dog and pinching its flesh in his bill.  The dog yelped and fell backwards as Duckworth moved forward beating his wings against the dog.

"Get out of here!" Andy roared. "Go home!"

The dog quickly backed off with its tail between its legs and ran away. Pugsley was still fighting to get away.

"It's okay, Pugsley, settle down," Sara said in a soothing voice.

"I didn't know a duck could fight off a dog like that," Andy said proudly. "That was so cool!"

"You were a good duck, protecting your buddy like that," Sara said looking affectionately at Duckworth.

"You were lucky to have such a good web-footed friend," Andy sighed. Sara and

Andy carried Pugsley all the way home with Duckworth waddling behind them.

## Chapter Eleven
## **The Lazy Days of Summer**

One day, after Andy delivered his flyers, Matt came over to jump on the trampoline.

"The summer holidays are nearly half over," Andy said sadly.

"I can't believe how fast it goes," Matt replied. "Before you know it, school will be starting."

"We've had so much fun with Duckworth this summer, it's going to be hard to go back," Andy sighed.

"Why don't we take Duckworth down the bike path to the pond tomorrow?" Matt suggested.

"Okay," Andy said. "We can put Duckworth in the wagon I use for flyers."

"When do you want to leave," asked Matt.

"Be here at ten o'clock and bring a lunch," Andy answered.

"Okay. See you tomorrow, Andy."

The boys left as planned, pulling Duckworth in the wagon. It took them at least a half an hour to get to the pond because Duckworth kept jumping out of the wagon. The pond wasn't very large. It was surrounded by tall bulrushes and interesting rocks. There were lots of frogs and salamanders, and sometimes, if you were lucky, you could even see a muskrat. Today, there were several ducks swimming in the pond.

"Hey, we can introduce Duckworth to the other ducks," Andy said.

"What kind of ducks are they?" Matt asked.

"They are Mallards," Andy replied. "A long time ago in China, people started to raise Mallard ducks. They bred them for certain colors and sizes. After many years they were able to produce several different types of ducks. The Peking duck is one of them."

"So, in other words, Duckworth is a distant relative," Matt stated.

"Right," Andy nodded. "Come on, Duckworth. You can really swim in here."

Duckworth had already jumped out of the wagon and was waddling slowly down to the pond. He took a drink, and then pushed off into the water, swimming only a few feet from the shore.

"Why won't he go further?" Matt asked. "Maybe he wants to stay close to me," Andy replied.

"I'll keep him here," Matt suggested. "You run across to the other side of the pond, and then call him. Let's see if he will swim over."

Matt waded out into the water to keep Duckworth from following Andy. When Andy reached the other side of the pond, he called.

"Here, Duckworth. Here, ducky."

Duckworth turned to Andy and swam right across towards him. When the duck was halfway to Andy, Andy ran back to where Matt stood and called again.

"Here, Duckworth."

Duckworth turned and swam toward Andy again.

"I am sure no one will believe this," Andy said.

"Look, the other ducks are swimming over to check out Duckworth," Matt commented.

"I bet they've never seen a duck like him before," Andy said. "They're small compared to Duckworth."

As soon as Duckworth saw the other ducks were getting closer, he quickly swam to shore and waddled out of the pond.

"He doesn't want anything to do with them," Andy said.

"Do you think it's because they're not the same color?" Matt asked.

"He's probably scared and doesn't know what they are," Andy replied.

"Right," Matt agreed. "He's never seen a duck before!"

"I don't think Duckworth even knows that he is a duck!" Andy exclaimed.

The Mallard ducks lost interest in Duckworth and swam away. The boys ate their sandwiches and tossed their crusts in the pond for Duckworth. After playing in the water and catching some frogs, they loaded Duckworth into the wagon. He must have been tired because this time he didn't try to jump out.

"That was a fun day," said Andy. Matt nodded, "What should we do tomorrow?"

Soon it was the middle of August. Andy went away with his family to visit his Grandparents at their summer cottage. He hated to leave Duckworth, but Mom and Dad decided the trip was too long to bring him. Ryan stayed home to work and to take care of the animals.  Andy loved to go to the cottage because it was on a lake.  This year the weather was perfect, but he missed Duckworth.  Andy called home regularly to see how he was doing.  Andy was happy when it was time to go home even though it meant school would start soon.  As soon as Andy arrived home, he rushed into the back yard.

"Hey, Duckworth," Andy called.  The duck ran out from under the deck and waddled in circles around Andy.  "I missed you too." Andy said.  He sat on the steps of the deck and told Duckworth all about the lake.  Suddenly Andy stopped.  "Something is different," he said looking at Duckworth.  "You sound different."

"Wongh, wongh."
"Are you quacking?"
"Wongh, wongh," Duckworth nodded.

"You are." Andy ran across the deck and yelled into the kitchen. "Hey, everyone, come here. Duckworth is quacking!"

It was too hot to sleep in the house that night, so Andy made a bed on the trampoline. Looking up as the sun set, Andy watched the cotton candy clouds stretch across the sky and change color, from orange, to pink, then to purple. He looked over at Duckworth affectionately. He was standing on the rock in his pool.

"We sure had fun this summer," Andy sighed.

Duckworth quacked and nodded his head.

## Chapter Twelve
## **Back to School**

Andy wished he could be as excited about going back to school as Matt was when he came over the next day.

"Finally, we are going to be the oldest kids in the school," Matt exclaimed as he watched Andy clean out Duckworth's pool.

"Yeah, but grade six is also the hardest grade," Andy complained. "There will be a lot more homework, which means I will have less time to spend with Duckworth."

"He'll be fine. He was happy to swim in his pool and eat the grass with Pugsley while you were at the lake." Matt reminded him.

"What's going to happen when the weather gets cold?" Andy asked. "Pugsley won't be outside anymore. The pool will be frozen. How's he supposed to keep warm?"

"Can't he live in the house for the winter?" Matt asked.

"No way," Andy shook his head, filling the pool with fresh water. "That won't work. He's just too messy. Mom's already talking about giving him away."

"You'd better think of something," Matt remarked.

"I know," Andy sighed. Duckworth noticed the pool was full and waddled in beating his wings on the water. Andy and Matt ran away before they got soaked.

The first day of school was actually fun for Andy. It was good to see all his friends again. Most of them asked about Duckworth. Best of all, Miss Reed was going to be his grade six teacher!

"Bring Duckworth in for a visit sometime," she urged. "We would all like to see him again."

"Sure," Andy said. "That will be fun."

Andy was right; he had a lot of homework! The weeks passed by quickly with projects to do, tests to study for, and his flyer route. Andy's time with Duckworth was limited, but Duckworth seemed very content regardless.

By the middle of October, Duckworth's pool started to freeze over. Winter was expected to come early. Pugsley stayed inside the house to sleep at night. She let everyone know that she was not happy inside by thumping her feet throughout the night until morning when Sara put her outside for the day.

Andy felt sorry for Duckworth. He was really dirty and hadn't been able to take a bath for a couple of weeks. One day after school Andy carried Duckworth upstairs.

"I know I should wait to ask Mom," Andy explained to Duckworth, "but she might say no. We'll be finished before she gets home."

Duckworth wasn't sure about the whole idea, but as soon as the tub was full, Duckworth started splashing. He darted around the tub, diving under the surface, and then beating the water with his wings. Andy was soaked, but he didn't care. He loved to watch him bathe. The duck swam back and forth pulling all the shampoo bottles into the tub. Andy laughed. Duckworth looked just like a kid with a bunch of rubber duckies.

Andy let the water out of the tub. Duckworth was drying off and preening his feathers.

"I'm going to get some old towels to mop up all this water. I'll be right back."

While Andy was in the laundry room, he heard Sara scream. He raced back into the bathroom. Duckworth was sitting on the edge of the tub. He quacked and nodded at Andy as he entered.

"My new Cashmere sweater," Sara whined. "Look what your duck has done!" she yelled.

Sara's sweater lay in the bottom of the tub, soaking up the grime from Duckworth's bath. She pulled her sweater out from under all the shampoo bottles.

"Hey, what's happening?" Ryan asked entering the bathroom. Duckworth quacked and nodded. "Why is the duck in here?"

"My sweater is ruined," Sara cried. "Why is the duck in here?"

"I just left him for a minute to dry off," Andy tried to explain.

"My clothes were still in here. Why couldn't you wait until I was finished?" Sara demanded.

"I thought that you were," Andy replied.

"She's never finished," Ryan said. "She's always preening!"

"What's the problem here?" Dad asked walking in. Duckworth quacked and nodded. "Why is the duck in here?"

"My sweater was hanging off the shower curtain so the wrinkles would fall out..."

"...and Duckworth pulled it in." Dad finished her sentence.

"It's not the end of the world, is it?" Ryan asked sarcastically.

Mom rushed into the bathroom. "What's going on?" Duckworth quacked and nodded. "Why is the duck in here?

"Look at my new sweater," Sara cried.

"Can it be cleaned?" Dad asked calmly.

"No," Sara moaned.

"Why is the duck in the bathroom?" Mom asked impatiently.

"Duckworth needed a bath," Andy yelled. "His pool is frozen."

"Don't raise your voice at your Mother!" Dad scolded.

"Man, this sure seems like a lot more 'duck' than it's 'worth'," Ryan commented. Duckworth quacked and nodded.

## Chapter Thirteen
## A Trip to the Farm

  Sara finally settled down when Andy agreed to buy her a new sweater. Luckily, he was able to expand his flyer route to earn more money. He should have asked before letting Duckworth take a bath. Andy was nervous that the 'family feud' would have lasting effects, maybe even lessening his chances to keep Duckworth.

  One day in late October when walking out of school, Andy saw his Mom's car waiting in the parking lot. He ran up to greet her then noticed Duckworth in a box in the front seat. Andy's heart sank. He knew the dreaded day had come.

"Where are we going?" he asked as he climbed into the car.

"I found a duck farm to take Duckworth to," Mom said.

"For the winter?" Andy asked.

"Well, no," Mom hesitated. "I guess it will be his new home."

"Mom, do we have to?" Andy pleaded trying to hold back the tears.

"What else can we do?" Mom asked. "I'm sure he will be happy there. What better place is there for duck than on a duck farm?"

Duckworth was very quiet and obviously upset. His wings were flared out slightly at the top as he panted through his partially opened bill.

Andy sat stunned, holding Duckworth for what might be the last time. The rest of the ride was quiet except for the music playing on the radio. Thirty minutes later, they pulled into the 'The Dapper Duck Farm'.

"It looks really nice here," Mom said. They got out of the car and Andy carried Duckworth through the gate towards the house.

"That must be Mr. Smith," Mom said pointing to the man in the overalls and rubber boots. "He's expecting us."

Andy put Duckworth down and he waddled close behind him.

"Hi, I'm Helen. This is my son, Andy. I believe I spoke to you on the phone."

"Ah yes, and this is the duck," Mr. Smith said.

"His name is Duckworth," Andy said nervously.

"He's a nice-looking drake. See how his tail curves up with those curly feathers on it? That shows that he's a male. I would guess he's about six months old, but he's larger than most."

"How many ducks do you have here?" Andy asked

"Right now, probably around five hundred."

"Wow," Mom said. "Where do you keep them all?"

"Is there a pond for them to swim in?" Andy added.

"There are several fields where I let them run, and a couple of large barns for shelter.

They keep pretty warm when they're all together," Mr. Smith said. "And there's a large water trough with plenty of fresh water."

"What do you do with all of them?" Andy questioned.

"Well," Mr. Smith hesitated, "We're in the business of...raising ducks."

Andy was confused. "But what will you do with Duckworth?"

"You can leave him right here," he said.

Andy panicked. "Now?"

"Feel free to walk around if you'd like. He'll be fine here. When you leave, just make sure to close the gate on your way out. I'll move him into one of the other fields later tonight," Mr. Smith instructed. He turned and went into the house.

Beside the house was an open pasture with a small flock of ducks and a variety of different animals. It looked like the perfect place for a duck all right, but Andy could tell that Duckworth was not going to fit in. He looked like a city duck coming to meet his country cousins. Andy imagined Duckworth wearing a top hat and tails, impeccably groomed without a feather out of place, standing tall as he walked, nodding politely to passersby with a regal air. His country cousins, on the other hand, were scruffy, dirty, and walked slouched over.

"Let's go walk him around to help him get acquainted with his new surroundings," Mom suggested.

Andy walked into the pasture with Duckworth following at his heels.

"Look at the cute goats," Mom said. Duckworth lowered his head and puffed up his feathers.

"I bet they remind him of the dog he met in the ravine." Andy explained walking over to the ducks.

"Look, Duckworth, they're Peking ducks, just like you," Andy said. Duckworth looked terrified and ran the other way.

"He seems more afraid of the ducks than he was of the goats," Mom said, with a confused look.

Andy felt sicker and sicker about leaving Duckworth. Off in the corner of the field, Andy saw a rabbit.

"Look, a bunny," Andy said relieved. "There is something you will recognize. Come on Duckworth, you can hang out with him." Andy walked towards the rabbit. "See the bunny?" Andy asked. Duckworth was not interested and stayed between Andy's feet.

"I think we should go now," Mom said. "Once we're gone, I'm sure he will settle down."

"What if he doesn't?" Andy asked as tears filled his eyes.

" He will," Mom said, trying to reassure Andy. "It may just take some time." But she didn't sound so sure herself.

Duckworth followed Andy and Mom all the way back to the front gate.

"Mom, he knows that we're going to leave him here. We can't do it," Andy pleaded. "Please Mom, let's just take him home."

"No, Andy," Mom insisted. "This is the best place for him." She opened the gate in the wire fence and rushed through before Duckworth could get there. "Quick!" she yelled.

"I'm sorry, Duckworth," Andy said pushing him so he could squeeze through the gate. Mom shut it just in time, locking Duckworth on the other side.

"It's okay, Duckworth." Andy said putting his hand through the wire to stroke his head for the last time. Andy choked back tears. "You'll be fine here with all the other ducks."

"Andy, let's go," Mom called from the car.

"Bye, ducky" Andy sobbed. He wiped the tears from his eyes and slowly dragged himself to the car and pulled himself inside. Duckworth quacked frantically and tried to find a way to get under the fence. Then he started searching for a way around the fence. As they drove away, Andy glanced back to take one last look. To his horror, he saw Duckworth running along the entire length of the wire fence after their car. Andy cried all the way home.

## Chapter Fourteen
## **Winter Quarters**

It was on the drive home that Andy decided he would somehow get Duckworth back. That night, he hardly slept. He couldn't get the thought of Duckworth racing after the car out of his mind. Judging from the way Mom looked this morning, she must have had a similar night.

Andy's eyes were still red and puffy when he walked to school the next morning. He left early to go to the library before the bell rang. He signed out a book about building poultry shelters. He studied it all day in class when the teacher wasn't looking.

"Are you sick or something?" Matt asked on the way home. "You look terrible."

"No," Andy said fighting back tears.

"Has something happened to Duckworth?" Matt asked.

Andy nodded. "He's gone."

"GONE!" Matt exclaimed. "Gone where?"

"Some duck farm but I'm going to get him back," Andy said as he opened the gate to his backyard.

"Let me know if there's anything I can do to help," Matt said. "I mean anything."

Andy walked through the yard. It was dead quiet. There was no duck quacking or nodding to greet him. He trudged into the house. No one was home so he went upstairs to his room and fell asleep.

Andy was dreaming that he was running through the sprinkler with Duckworth. Suddenly the sprinkler turned into Mr. Smith's face and it waved wildly on the end of the hose. Andy thrashed around in his bed.

"Run, Duckworth! Run!" he yelled.

"Andy! Wake up," Mom nudged him gently. "It's only a dream."

Andy sat up. Tears filled his eyes. "That's the trouble, Mom. This is not just a dream."

Everyone was seated at the table when Andy and Mom came down.

Andy wasn't hungry. Supper was unusually quiet until Andy broke the silence.

"Mom. Dad, we need to get Duckworth back."

"Here we go again," Ryan said impatiently.

"But how can we take care of him during the winter?" Mom asked.

Dad sighed, "We've been over this before."

"I'd be upset if I had to give away Pugsley," Sara sympathized.

"Maybe something has already happened to Duckworth," Ryan said.

"What do you mean?" Andy asked.

"What does Farmer Smith raise all those ducks for?" Ryan questioned.

"I asked him but..." a horrified look came across Andy's face. "Does he raise them to eat?"

"What else are you going to do with 500 ducks!" Ryan answered.

All the color drained from Andy's face. Seeing his reaction, Ryan looked as if he were sorry for what he'd said.

"Mom, how can you do this?" Sara asked.

"I thought a duck farm would be a good place for a duck," Mom said sadly.

"Please stop and listen to me," Andy begged. "I got this book out of the library today. It tells you how to build a poultry shelter." He showed the plans to his Dad and Ryan.

"This is a lot of work, Andy," Dad said, looking over the plans. "How would we pour cement for the foundation and the floor?"

"The book says that cinderblocks can be used for both, instead." Andy explained.

"The cement would be cold," Mom said, "and how would you clean it?"

"The cinderblocks are dug six inches into the ground. The shelter sits on top of it. The floor is removable. It is made of wire mesh. That's so a lot of the mess can fall through onto the ground."

"That's an interesting design," Dad commented.

Andy flipped the page of the book and pointed to a picture.

"See the nesting box or sleeping box. It is placed in the corner and filled with wood chips that can be changed often. Every few weeks you remove the floor and shovel out underneath."

"This window looks tricky," Dad said.

"It would be warmer without a window," Mom said. "You could put in a special grow light instead, the kind I use for my plants in the greenhouse."

"A light?" Ryan asked. "That means you need electricity."

"That's easy," Dad said. "We could install an outlet inside the shelter."

"How about heating it?" Andy asked.

"Hum," Dad pondered. "What about an in-car-heater? It could be attached to a thermostat which could be set to whatever temperature you want."

"So, when the temperature drops below what you have set, the heater will turn on, just like in our house," Ryan said.

"The outlet and the thermostat can both be powered by running an extension cord from the outlet on the deck," Dad explained.

"Sounds great," Andy said enthusiastically.

"That's some pretty high-tech winter quarters for a duck," Ryan added.

"When the really cold weather hits, Duckworth would have to stay in there day and night. Would he be happy?" Mom inquired.

"Well, I was thinking, if its ok with Sara, Pugsley could live in the shelter too," Andy suggested.

"I think Pugsley would like that," Sara agreed. "She isn't happy anymore living inside the house. I think she misses Duckworth."

"How much will all this cost? Mom asked.

"We'd only need cinderblocks, wood, insulation, and shingles for the roof," Andy replied.

"I have an old heater we could use," Dad said. "I bet we could make it for a hundred dollars.

"I have that much money in the bank," Andy said.

"I thought we agreed that money was for university," Mom reminded him.

Andy needed to think of something fast. "I'll rake leaves this weekend," he said. "Matt will help me. If we rake five yards and charge twenty dollars per yard that would be a hundred dollars."

"That will be a lot of work," Mom said.

"I can do it," Andy said enthusiastically. "Can Duckworth come home?"

"What do you think, Helen?" asked Dad

"Let's talk again, once you have the money."

## Chapter Fifteen
## Home Sweet Home

As soon as supper was over, Andy excused himself from the table and went directly to phone Matt. He agreed to come over at nine o'clock the next morning with his rake.

Saturday was a perfect fall day. The boys had no trouble finding five yards to rake. They soon learned that raking leaves was a lot harder and took way longer than either of them had anticipated. They worked all day until it was nearly dusk. The two tired and dirty boys sat on the back deck, counting the money.

"We did it!" Andy said. "We made one hundred and ten dollars."

"How did that happen?" Matt asked as he looked at his blisters.

"Mr. Blumell felt sorry for us and gave us a ten-dollar tip. I can't wait to tell Mom and Dad. Now I can get Duckworth back," he cheered.

"I should go," Matt said getting up slowly.

"Thanks Matt," Andy said. "I couldn't have done it without you."

"You owe me," Matt teased.

Andy rushed into the house. The rest of the family had just finished supper.

"When can we go get Duckworth?" Andy asked waving the money in the air.

"You made that much money in one day?" Ryan asked in shock.

"It was a very long day," Andy replied as he mopped the sweat off his dirty forehead.

"Good job, Andy," Mom said.

Dad gave Andy a manly pat on the back. "I'm proud of you son."

"When can we go?" Andy asked impatiently.

"You're sure you want to do this?" Mom questioned. "It's going to be a lot of work cleaning the shelter."

"I'll help him," Sara offered. "Pugsley will be living there too."

"You're not going to change your mind?" Mom asked.

"How about you sleep on it, Andy?" Dad said. "If you feel the same in the morning, you can call Mr. Smith."

First thing the next morning, Andy made the call.

"Hi, Mr. Smith, this is Andy Johnson. I've changed my mind about giving you my duck. I wonder if I could come by this morning and pick him up?"

"Oh, the Peking duck?" Mr. Smith asked.

"Yes," Andy said quickly. "His name is Duckworth."

"You just left him a few days ago and now you want him back?" Mr. Smith asked puzzled.

"Yes, is that ok?" Andy asked.

"Are you going to change your mind again?" Mr. Smith questioned.

"No, I won't. Not this time." Andy wasn't sure if he was teasing or not.

"All right, I'll be here all day," Mr. Smith said.

"Thanks. Bye." Andy hung up the phone. "YES!"

Everyone, except Ryan, decided to go for a nice Sunday drive in the country to pick up Duckworth. The trip was much happier this time. Dad pulled up in front of the farm. Andy jumped out of the car before it came to a complete stop.

"I don't see Duckworth," Andy thought. He ran up to the house and rang the doorbell.

"I wonder where he is." Andy looked impatiently through the opened screen door. He noticed a wooden plaque, in the shape of a duck, hanging on the wall. He moved a little closer to see what it said.

Andy stepped back. "Ryan was right," he thought. "I hope I'm not too late." Finally, Mr. Smith came to the door.

"Hi, I've come to get Duckworth," Andy blurted out.

"Okay," Mr. Smith said. "I'll take you out to the field, but I don't know how you are going to find him."

They followed Mr. Smith through the pasture, towards a large building.

"The duck didn't want to stay in the pasture," he said. "He kept finding a way to get back to the house." Mr. Smith opened the gate to a large open field.

"He's over there in that field with about two hundred other ducks," he said pointing to the large flock. "Good luck finding him."

Andy walked into the field with his Mom, Dad, and Sara behind him.

"Duckworth," Andy called.

The flock started running. Andy's heart raced. He'd never seen so many ducks. There were hundreds of them.

"Duckworth, here ducky," Andy called again. "How am I going to find him," he cried.

Everyone walked into the field calling to Duckworth.

"Maybe he's not here," Andy said anxiously.

"I'm sure he's here somewhere," Mom said sounding a little nervous.

"Maybe Mr. Smith took us to the wrong field," Sara said.

"Or maybe he's gone like Ryan said," Andy fought back the tears.

"Let's not panic," Dad said calmly. "Keep calling."

"Duckworth," they all called.

Andy saw Mr. Smith watching from a distance. Then, out of the corner of his eye, Andy spotted one duck that looked different than the rest. He stood tall, with his head up. Andy turned slightly to get a better look. Just then, the duck broke away from the rest of the ducks and ran towards Andy!

"It's him!" Andy shouted. "Here, Duckworth!"

Then, for Andy, everything went in slow motion like some commercials on T.V. Duckworth ran towards Andy and Andy ran towards Duckworth. Even though he was dirty, with his feathers out of place, he still looked regal. Finally, the two met in the middle of the field.

"Duckworth," Andy cried as the duck ran into his arms. "I'm here to take you home."

Mom, Dad and Sara ran to greet Andy and Duckworth as Mr. Smith stood at a distance shaking his head in disbelief.

"He's so happy to see us," Andy said as they drove home in the car. "Listen to him, he won't stop quacking."

"I bet he's telling us about all his adventures on the farm," Mom sighed.

Andy sat back and finally relaxed. He imagined what Duckworth might be saying..."

"I can't believe you left me at that farm! What were you thinking? Do you know what I've been through? Look at me! I'm a mess. I don't think I've ever been this dirty. Besides that, I'm starving. I haven't eaten since you left me here. I could never get near the food, with all the pushing and shoving. They really are uncivilized. Home sweet home! I can't wait to get there! By the way, how is Pugsley? She's not going to believe any of this either! Do you think I can have a bath as soon as we get home? I think it's the least you can do, after what I've been through..."

## Chapter Sixteen
## The Christmas Duck

Andy took Duckworth upstairs to take a bath as soon as they got home. Duckworth was so happy to get into the water. Andy made sure he was completely dry before taking him outside, even though it wasn't very cold.

Dad and Andy worked every night on the shelter for a couple of weeks. Andy was the 'gopher'. His job was to go for whatever Dad needed. Ryan helped when they needed an extra pair of hands. The shelter was finished just before the first snow. It was perfect. Duckworth and Pugsley enjoyed being together and Andy was finally able to relax and concentrate on his schoolwork.

A few weeks later, Andy made arrangements to take Duckworth to school.

"I can't believe how big he has grown," Miss Reed remarked. "He's so beautiful."

Mr. Sanders stopped briefly outside the classroom door. Andy was relieved when he decided not to come in.

Everyone crowded around Duckworth. He seemed to love all the attention. Miss Reed asked the class to sit down.

"We are really lucky to have Duckworth with us today," she said. "Now that you have all had a chance to see Duckworth, does anyone have any questions they would like to ask Andy?"

The class asked all the usual questions that you would expect.  How much does Duckworth weigh?  When did he start to quack?  What is his favorite thing to eat?

"I have a question for you Andy," Miss Reed said.  "What is the most important thing that you have learned while taking care of Duckworth?"

Andy thought for a minute. "I had no idea it was going to be so much work."  He thought back to cleaning the deck.  "Sometimes I just wanted to quit but I had to think about Duckworth.  I learned that when you make a commitment, you can't just give up when it gets hard."

"You're absolutely right," Miss Reed said.  "Sometimes it takes people a long time to learn that."

"Miss Reed, there is something else I would like to say."

"Go ahead, Andy," Miss Reed encouraged.

"As much as I have enjoyed having Duckworth, I don't think it is right to hatch ducklings for school projects.  He doesn't know how to be a duck.  That isn't right.  He only knows how to be a pet. I wonder what happens to all the other animals that are used for school projects."

"That is a very good point, Andy," Miss Reed said. "I think it should be brought up for discussion with the school board."

Old Man Winter had definitely arrived, and he brought along his good friend Jack Frost. They were both busy working their magic. Andy studied the intricate pattern of frost on the kitchen window. He glanced across the deck to the new shelter. It was sprinkled with frost and glistened in the rays of the sun. Andy smiled knowing that Duckworth and

Pugsley were warm and cozy inside, no matter how cold it was outside.

Every day after school, Andy and Sara would check the wood chips in the sleeping box, remove any dirty ones then sprinkle a new layer of wood chips on top. Then they filled up the water and food dishes. After about a month they would remove the floor to shovel everything out and then start again.

On warmer days, Andy let Duckworth and Pugsley out of the shelter for a few hours. Duckworth didn't like the snow. Immediately he would lie down, tucking his feet into the pocket-like folds on the sides of his body. Pugsley loved to play in the snow and ran circles around Duckworth.

When it was really cold, Duckworth and Pugsley came inside for a visit. Duckworth would have a bath, and then stay in Andy's old play pen for a few hours.

Andy was very busy at school which made the days and weeks pass quickly. Before long, school was finished for the Christmas holidays. When it was warm enough Andy and Matt took Duckworth tobogganing in the ravine and skating on the pond.

On Christmas day, after all the presents were opened, Andy brought Duckworth in the house for a visit. For his Christmas gift, Andy took him upstairs to have a long and luxurious bath in the tub. For a little extra Christmas cheer, Andy threw a few leaves of lettuce on top of the water for Duckworth to eat.

While Duckworth was drying off, Andy made a bow with ribbon from one of the presents. He tied it around Duckworth's neck.

"You look so festive, Duckworth," Andy said, stepping back to get a better look. "After supper, I'll take a picture of you standing beside the Christmas tree."

Andy carried Duckworth downstairs, then put him onto the floor. He peeked around the corner into the kitchen. Everyone was already seated at the table.

"We have a special guest this year for Christmas dinner," Andy announced proceeding down the hall. Duckworth followed behind, quacking softly.

"May I present the Christmas Duck!"
"Oh, look at his bow," Sara chuckled.
"Isn't that just ducky," Ryan teased.

"Before we eat," Andy said. "I would like to thank all of you for being so understanding and for helping me with Duckworth. It means a lot to me..."

Duckworth quacked and nodded. Everyone laughed.

"...and to Duckworth," Andy added.

"He's a very handsome Christmas duck," Mom said.

"Thankfully, he's not the kind of Christmas duck that Mr. Sanders had in mind!" Andy said and smiled.    The End

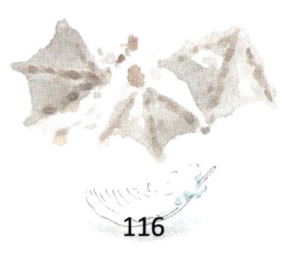

# About the Author

Marilyn Sabey lives in Calgary, Alberta with her husband and four-pound Yorkie, Miss Charlie. Marilyn enjoys hiking, bike riding, cross country skiing and kayaking, all with Miss Charlie by her side or riding in a pouch.

After a brief career as a Registered Respiratory Therapist, Marilyn decided to stay home to raise her four children.

Marilyn has always had a passion for the outdoors. As a young girl, she took care of many wild animals and pets. She taught her children to appreciate nature as they spent every day together exploring the ravine and park lands where they lived.

In 2005, Marilyn completed a yearlong correspondence course, "Writing for Children and Teenagers", from the Institute of Children's Literature and a three-month course, "Writing for Children", from the Alberta College of Art.

Once retired, Marilyn hopes to publish several of her magazine articles about animals, and write another children's book entitled, "The Adventures of Grandma Lyn."

## About the Illustrator

Jennifer Young lives in Calgary with her husband, dog, snake etc. ...

This is Jennifer's first time illustrating a Children's book, thanks to the ample free time provided by the 2020 pandemic.

Jennifer is a 1986 graduate of the Alberta College of Art and Design.  Upon graduating, she worked as a graphic artist at a glassware decorating company.  Later, Jennifer developed her own line a cartoon horse calendars and t-shirts, inspired from owning horses.  Who owned who, however, was up for debate.

Jennifer is a nature and animal nut, surrounding herself with all manner of critters, rescues wild and tame.  Who is wild or tame, however, is also up for debate.

Made in the USA
Middletown, DE
28 November 2020